EARLY PRAISE F

LOVE IT FORWARD

"*Love It Forward* offers readers delicious wisdom and uplifting insights about everyday life and what really matters, like love, for instance. This book is delightful."

—CAROLINE MYSS, Author of *Anatomy of the Spirit* and *Sacred Contracts*

"An exciting, vibrant, juicy, challenging book by one of our bravest and most illumined writers, a Lion in the making."

—ANDREW HARVEY, author of *The Hope: A Guide to Sacred Activism*

"Jeff Brown 'loves it forward' simply by sharing these poignant reflections about the ways in which we stay true to our human destinies. His novel use of language invites us to reconsider suppositions we have long ago put to bed. Time to awaken them again and view them with the transforming eyes of love. Jeff helps me believe in-deed that "love is all you need.""

—FATHER EDWARD L. BECK, CNN Faith and Religion Contributor and author of *God Underneath*

"I am in love with this book and profoundly inspired to hug every person I see on my path. Humanity has come so far in so many ways, but it's time to remember the most important piece of our puzzle - Love. *Love it Forward* is a beautiful, inspiring, and insightful gift to lead us back to the place we belong. In love with ourselves, with each other and with our planet.

> —BETSY CHASSE, co-creator '*What the bleep do we know?!*' and author of *Tipping Sacred Cows*

"*Love it Forward* is a wise and playful book that illuminates the bewildering corners of spiritual growth with a bright and joyful light."

> —BARNET BAIN, producer *What Dreams May Come*, *The Celestine Prophecy*

"*Love It Forward* contains lots of fascinating, touching and inspiring ideas to contemplate and 'soak in'. It's valuable for us to be focussing our thought and emotions on love and a loving intention. You are sure to find many uplifting quotes that resonate deep within you."

> —INNA SEGAL, creator of Visionary Intuitive Healing®; author of *The Secret Language of Your Body* and *The Secret of Life Wellness*

"What I love about Jeff Brown is his ability to remind us to stop seeking enlightenment and some mystical "out there" experience, but to experience what he calls "enrealment," the power of being truly human, in this world, on this earth, right now, directly with each other while staying aligned with our soul's path. *Love it Forward* is a wonderful feast of what seems to me the most important work we can each be doing on the planet right now---learning how to love ourselves and each other."

—JAYSON GADDIS, relational warrior
(www.JaysonGaddis.com)

"*Love It Forward* -- what a concept! Author Jeff Brown, known for his spiritual word-o-matics, entices his reader with this open-to-any-page book to embrace Love, then pass the intrinsic emotion forward to encircle the planet. Jeff, keep making love with the Divine; keep writing to share your heart consciousness with humanity, we will read what you pen!"

—BARBARA SINOR, PH.D., author of
The Pact: Messages from the Other Side

"Jeff's raw, resonant words will melt your heart open. *Love it forward* is a tender, spicy collection of kindling sure to ignite the flames of your soul. With familiar grace, his organic voice invites us to recognize each other by heart, remembering that we really are the love we seek. A precious book to keep close by for nourishing everyday visits, and just as divine to share and love forward."

—JESSIE MAY WOLFE *(www.jessiemay.com)*

"Jeff Brown's intellect and wit shines throughout his writing. He dives deeply into his own heart to harvest pearls of wisdom that speak to our common humanity. His thoughts are like mirrors that invite us to heal anything that is preventing us from becoming our most authentic selves. He is able to express profound truths that can elicit a tear and a smile simultaneously. His words are a gift to anyone who has embraced life as a spiritual journey: a reminder that "love is all there is."

—DR. KATHIA LASZLO, Systems Theorist,
Saybrook Graduate School

LOVE IT FORWARD

Jeff Brown

ENREALMENT PRESS
TORONTO, CANADA

Published by Enrealment Press
PO Box 64
Acton, Ontario
Canada L7J 2M2

Cover photo by Andrekart Photography/Shutterstock
Author photo by Paul Hemrend
Cover and book design by Allyson Woodrooffe (go-word.com)
Printed in the USA

Library and Archives Canada Cataloguing in Publication
Brown, Jeff, 1962-, author
Love it forward / Jeff Brown.

Issued in print and electronic formats.
ISBN 978-0-9808859-3-4 (pbk.)
ISBN 978-0-9808859-4-1 (pdf)

1. Brown, Jeff, 1962- --Quotations. 2. Love--Quotations,
maxims, etc. 3. Spiritual life--Quotations, maxims, etc. I. Title.
PN6084.L6B76 2014   302.3   C2013-907749-9
                                  C2013-907750-2

This book is dedicated to my father, Albert Ronald Brown, who recently passed. His love for the healing power of the written word lives on in me. I love him forward with all that I write, both healing the rifts between us and giving voice to his soul on its journey through time.

Preface
Loving It Forward...

 M y father passed away this summer. It had been some time since we had talked...too long perhaps...but it always feels like that after someone dies. You yearn for a little more time with them- to clear the debris, to soften the edges, to find the love.

My father Albert was a mix of tender poetry and volatile outbursts. Like many men of his generation, he was trapped between his duties as a provider and his brilliant inner life. What he most wanted was to become a writer, one who wrote of spiritual matters, the meaning of life, the deeper path. He couldn't quite get there- as his circumstances and issues blocked his expression- but his intentions were passed on to me, one generation later. In his own unique way, he passed me the karmic baton, loving his calling forward to the next generation. And on it goes.

When I think of my life, I think of all that has been loved forward: the grandparents who nurtured me, the English teacher who validated me, the strangers that smiled at me, the lovers who held me, the readers who encouraged me to write on. So many acts of love that landed deep within me, strengthening me at the core, energizing me for the next steps on the journey. Even now, I feel many of my ancestors close at heart, sitting on my shoulder as I write these words, loving me onward. There is no doubt- I have been loved forward.

And so have you. You are here, now, because you have been loved forward. If not by fellow humans, then surely by Grace itself. That we are here means we are wanted here. It means we belong here. It is our life's work to uncover why. At the heart of this book is the belief that every individual came into this life with a sacred purpose at the core of their birth. We are not random concentrations of stardust, nor are we accidental tourists. We are divinely inspired, purposeful, and essential to this wondrous human tapestry. Although the ultimate romance is with our own soul, it is our experiences together that give birth to the essential lessons. If we get off the dance floor, we postpone others' lessons too.

This includes those who came before. When we love our gifts forward, we also love them backwards. In the survivalist world of generations past, it was rare for anyone to even identify their callings. It was all they could do to stay alive. When you actualize your gifts, you aren't just doing it for yourself. You are also doing it for all of the ancestors who were denied the opportunity to humanifest the treasures that lived within them. If you complete your task, however simple or humble it may be, you take them all to the next level. You breathe purpose for them, too.

And it's not only the actualization of our gifts that loves them backwards. It's also the healing of the heart. With every excavation of old material, with every clearing of our emotional debris, with every foray into a healthier way of being, we help to advance the collective heart as well. When we heal our wounds, we heal the world's wounds. If we listen closely, we will hear the spirits of the ancestors breathe a sigh of relief. We are never alone on the trailways of transformation.

When I was a university student, I discovered another way to love it forward. It began one afternoon when I was walking to class in downtown Toronto. A beggar stopped me and asked for change. At first, I was hesitant- too preoccupied with my own reality to absorb hers- but she persisted, looking deep into my eyes and asking again. I stopped, and looked deeply into her eyes. Whose eyes were these anyway? But for the Grace of God, they were my eyes, your eyes, the eyes of any member of the human race. But for the Grace of God and all of those who have loved you forward.

I gave her money. And then I gave money to a homeless man at the next corner. And then it became a habit. And then I got the bank account information for a homeless man in my area and made regular deposits to it. And then I began to make lunches for the homeless on Sunday afternoons. Although I didn't have words for it then, I intuitively knew that there was more to these interactions then met the eye(s). I was doing something for them, but they were also doing something for me. They were helping me to honor my calling to service, to be sure, but there was something else too...

A few years later, I befriended a homeless man called Slim while I was writing *Soulshaping*. We would sit on a city bench and discuss the difference between spiritual and physical homelessness. Although many of us had beautiful houses to live in- were we truly at home? Soon thereafter, Slim had the bright idea to sell my first edition of *Soulshaping* on the streets of Toronto. He stood on a downtown street corner with a red sweater that said "Buy a great self-help book here" and people flocked from everywhere to find him. In a matter of a few months, he sold hundreds and hundreds of books. He loved my writing forward, as I loved his efforts to re-join the world forward. It was a beautifully reciprocal relationship.

And then I understood. Unity consciousness is not simply a beautiful vision of possibility-it is our best and truest hope. Until each and every one of us rises into fullness, the collective cannot actualize its wholeness. Until we all rush to the side of someone in need, we are all fractured beings. Until we all recognize that each of us is a magnificent reflection of the Godself, we are collectively blind. Until everyone has what they need to flourish, we are all birds with one wing. The collective is only as healthy as its most challenged individual. Our community is humanity. We rise or fall in unison.

With this in heart, I launched the Love It Forward movement (www.loveitforward.net) on October 20, 2013 with my brilliant visionaries Amy Gallagher and Tarini Bresgi. Love It Forward is our best effort to co-create a paradigm for economic relations that benefits all members of the human family- not only a select few. By creating opportunities for those who are economically challenged, and by channeling profits to particular Love-In-Action causes, we practice the art of 'conscious capitalism'- inviting everyone to participate, and sharing the abundance with those in need. This is what we call 'wintentionality.' This book is one of the many products the movement will create and use as tools for bettering our world. A percentage of all profits from these product sales will go to sustaining and developing the movement.

Through benevolent eyes, the co-founders of Love It Forward recognize that the true warriors on the planet are those who have to overcome tremendous hardships with very little or no support. The real super-heroes are those that have been so disillusioned by the world, so uprooted in their daily life, yet they find a way to get up in the morning and believe in life again. We want to co-create a society that elevates and supports these individuals. We want to co-create a world that pulls humanity close, that refuses to let anyone fall off the edge, that breathes individuals back to life when they lose all hope, that moves the way loves makes us move. In this world of divine possibility, we will never forget that we are all part of this human-nest. If even one is left out, the nest is empty.

When I was young, I was in love with the beautiful French film 'The Red Balloon,' as was my father. The film captures the fascinating dynamic between a young boy and a sentient, silent, red balloon. I saw the balloon as a reflection of my own alienation. I wanted to connect with humanity, I trailed closely behind them, but I was often a little out of reach. And then, because I was different, because I was vulnerable in my isolation, I was trampled on by the collective. I can only imagine that this is how it feels to be a homeless person, or someone living on the edges of society. They want to be welcomed back, but they are afraid to be trampled on yet again. To love humanity forward is to embrace the red balloon in each of us. The cover image on this book is a testament to that vision of possibility.

Soon after my father's death, I had the most vivid dream. I was driving a car when I saw a truck hit my father. I got out to help him, but he was pinned under the truck. By the time I got around to the other side, he was sitting up on a stretcher. The paramedics were trying to save him. I intuitively knew that this was our chance to say goodbye. I got up behind him, put my hand on his lower back, and he turned to look right into my eyes. It was so deeply real. All I could say was "Let there be love Daddy, Let there be love." Repeatedly, like a mantra. He just looked at me, and smiled. Suddenly there was a beautiful black woman sitting a little above the stretcher smiling at me. She was an angel, no doubt there to take him home. And then I woke up. Not a moment later, thunder crashed through the night sky. I knew my father had finally made it home. Our tender goodbye moment had loved his soul forward.

When thinking of my father, I take comfort in these beautiful words, written by poet Susan Frybort:

> When I become heartbroken from a loved one's demise, I try to remember that life is fleeting for all and to love in the time

allotted. This, too, is a small comfort but one nevertheless. Because I know stars die all the time, and for each one that dies one is born. Life continues so love may endure.

May the sharings in this book help to love you forward in whatever way you need. Many of them arose as my Facebook status, spiritual graffiti that has touched other souls on their journey. At the back of the book are some longer writings, including 'You are Sacred Purpose' and some of the inspirations I wrote for ABC'S Good Morning America. I wrote a number of pieces for them, and was blessed to see them all loved forward as well.

Let there be love... Let there be love...

– Jeff Brown
Toronto, Canada
October 23, 2013

LOVE IT FORWARD

So many live their lives feeling unloved, unseen, unrecognized, unappreciated. So very many. You may not know who they are because we are all conditioned to hide our truth below a bushel of shame. But they are everywhere. When you make an effort to share your love, you don't always know where it will land. But be sure that it does. Sometimes it lights a torch for others to follow. Sometimes it gives them reason to believe that there is a better life waiting for them after a lifetime of disappointment. Sometimes it builds spirits and sometimes it actually saves lives. We just have to keep giving the love wherever and whenever we can. You never know how far it will travel.

♡

Words. So powerful. They can crush a heart, or heal it. They can shame a soul, or liberate it. They can shatter dreams, or energize them. They can obstruct connection, or invite it. They can create defenses, or melt them. We have to use words wisely.

♡

So called 'late-bloomers' get a bad rap. Sometimes the people with the greatest potential often take the longest to find their path because their sensitivity is a double edged sword- it lives at the heart of their brilliance, but it also makes them more susceptible to life's pains. Good thing we aren't being penalized for handing in our purpose late. The soul doesn't know a thing about deadlines.

♡

When we are young, it's the illusion of perfection that we fall in love with. As we age, it's the humanness that we fall in love with- the poignant stories of overcoming, the depthful vulnerability of aging, the struggles that grew us in karmic stature, the way a soul shaped itself to accommodate its circumstances. With less energy to hold up our armor, we are revealed and, in the revealing, we call out to each other's hearts. Where before wounds turned us off, they are now revealed as proof that God exists. Where we once saw imperfect scars, we now see evidence of a life fully lived.

♡

Out with the old, in with the true.

♡

We are all tired. Really, we are. It's a hard road, but it's also a beautiful one. Perhaps we expect too much from ourselves and from others. Perhaps humanity can only make slow progress, like an inchworm. Perhaps we need to celebrate how far we have come. And rest more. And relish the simple pleasures. And look for love everywhere. There is a river near where I live. It meanders slowly, peacefully. It doesn't ask itself why it isn't an ocean, or a raging river, or some other thing. It just surrenders to what it is. Maybe we just need to surrender more to who we are. I think I will lie down tomorrow beside the river. And take a rest. And sweet surrender.

♡

Everything real comes through the heart. When it is truly opened, everything secondary falls away- egoic glory, fame and fortune, substitute gratifications. The heart doesn't care about such things. It doesn't hold it against you if you don't own your own home, achieve your goals, have a perfect body. The heart doesn't care what you have earned or accumulated. No matter our seeming differences, we are all the same when the heart gate opens. Deep feeling levels the playing field. Love is the great equalizer.

♡

Excessive analysis perpetuates emotional paralysis. It's the heart that knows the path. The mind is just there to organize the steps.

♡

You can connect from all kinds of places- energetic harmony, sexual alchemy, intellectual alignment- but they won't sustain love over a lifetime. You need a thread that goes deeper, that moves below and beyond the shifting sands of compatibility. That thread is fascination- a genuine fascination with someone's inner world, with the way they organize reality, with the way they hearticulate their feelings, with the unfathomable and bottomless depths of their being. To hear their soul cry out to you again and again, and to never lose interest in what it is trying to convey. If there is that, then there will still be love when the body sickens, when the sexuality fades, when the perfection projection is long shattered. If there is that, you will swim in love's waters until the very last breath.

♡

If there is any need that is perpetually unmet on this planet, it is the need to feel seen. To feel seen in our humanity, in our vulnerability, in our beautiful imperfection. When we are held safe in that, a key turns inside of our hearts, freeing us from our isolation, transforming our inner world. If there is anything we can offer each other, it is the gift of sight. "I see you"- perhaps the most important words we can utter to another. I see you…

♡

One thing I have learned with certainty is not to stand in connection with those who diminish me. This is particularly difficult when family is involved, because we have a vested interest in perpetuating the family system for all kinds of different reasons. I don't believe one should endure abuse no matter how attached they are to an idea of family. There are many families (read: soulpod) waiting for us just outside our habitual awareness. We are not responsible for those who diminish us. We really have to get that. We can be compassionate and we can certainly understand where their abusiveness comes from, but understanding the origins does not mean we have to endure it. It's not our cross to bear.

♡

It's all too easy to give up, to stop believing, to turn away from the light. The evidence that the darkness will prevail is everywhere. But I am not persuaded. Because my heart keeps opening, because humans keep going, because the sun keeps rising. It may well be that we make it through by the narrowest of margins, but we will. This human spirit is unstoppable. This human heart is so beautiful, a phoenix that rises again and again from the ashes of indifference. We may only see glimpses of our divinity at this stage of development, but they are a harbinger of things to come. This unstoppable humannest. Such a majestic species.

♡

Standing in my dead father's apartment, cleaning it out, sifting through all his belongings and writings, one thing crystalizes in a way that transcends cliché. Savor every bloody moment of aliveness. Don't delay the delight to a day that may never come. Don't wait for the last breath before you wake the f*#k up. Savor every smile, every breeze, every kiss, every meal, every walk, every sleep, every sprinkle of faith. None of it is an illusion. It's all the real deal. Savor the gift of breath.

♡

We can't find our path without getting messy. Messy comes with the territory. We came in messy. We learn messy. We love messy. We leave messy. I never found my way to clarity without first befriending confusion, in all its chaotic forms. I never found a path that felt like home before falling into quicksand. I never established a new way of being without trying the wrong way of being on for size. I never found the light without stumbling around in the dark. I never tasted God before getting a little dirt in my mouth. In the heart of the chaos is the clay that shapes us home. Chaotic Magnificence!

♡

With respect to relationship, I believe that our best hope is to find our own sacred purpose, so that we are always making love with the divine. Then the question of relationship with another human takes on a different degree of meaning. We want it to enhance our lives, but not to make us whole.

♡

It is amazing what happens to your consciousness when you realize that you are the next generation up for dying. When my grandparents and both parents were still alive, I always felt like I had lots of time- time to waste, time to live, time to delay death consciousness- but since my Father died, my perspective has radically shifted. Now I am even more determined to create a life that is entirely true to path, that is deeply reflective of my gifts and callings, and that wastes no time on connections and patterns that don't serve. This is one of the gifts of loss. We realize how quickly we can go, and how precious every single moment is. We realize that it is time to stop seeking what we already know. We real-eyes that it is time to live.

♡

So many breakdown because they cannot carry the weight of falsity any longer. They are breaking through to a more authentic consciousness. Sadly, this is often stigmatized as a 'breakdown,' as though they are machines that stopped working. We need to up-frame these experiences and see them for what they are: break-throughs for inner freedom. At some point, we just can't carry the bullshit anymore and long to be real.

♡

Detachment is a tool – it's not a life.

♡

Sometimes people avoid the beginnings because they want to avoid the endings. This is particularly true if we have negative associations with happiness. If we have had the carpet pulled out from under us at moments of great vulnerability, we may prefer to avoid life altogether. But what is life without beginnings? Sure it may lead to sorrow, but it also may lead to joy. We must begin again, time and again, if we are going to live a real life.

♡

If you survive a hardship filled early life, if you make it through the faith canal relatively intact, you have something that only survivors can truly understand- a profound gratitude for every moment on the other side, a sense of relief that never leaves you, a wave of delight that doesn't take anything at all to ignite it. Suddenly, you are driving along, and you just feel so happy, because you are free, because you know the difference between doom and delight. When you have seen how ugly it can be, you appreciate every peaceful moment life offers. I am grateful that the universe kept me alive during my time in Family-Of-Origin Penitentiary, because I now appreciate every precious moment of freedom.

♡

When a lover runs away from us, we often take it deeply personal. But sometimes people run away because we are so wondrous that they can't take the reflection back to their own limitations. They aren't ready for wondrous yet...

♡

Our survival adaptations are so tough, but our wounds are so delicate. To heal, we have to lift the armor carefully- it saved our lives, after all. It's like moving your best friend off to the side of the path. You don't trample on her, you don't hit him with a sledgehammer. You honor her presence like a warm blanket that has kept you safe and sound during wintry times. And then, when the moment is right, you get inside and stitch your wounds with the thread of love, slowly and surely, not rushing to completion, nurturing as you weave, tender and true. The healing process has a heart of its own, moving at its own delicate pace. We are such wondrous weavers...

♡

Isn't it time we constructed a new language, one that is rooted in the yearning, the wisdom, the compassion, the softening of the receptive heart. The language of the mind can be very clever, but the language of the heart has a brilliance all its own. When we hearticulate, we speak from a place of essence, the place where God lives. What a bountiful dictionary- such subtle textures and tones, such a wondrous lexicon of hope. Let's hearticulate a new language- the language of love.

♡

Oh, what's the rush...
It takes a long time to clear emotional debris.
It takes a long time to peel off our armor.
It takes a long time to recognize our magnificence.
It takes a long time to heal our shame.
It takes a long time to explore our possibilities.
It takes a long time to find our voice.
It takes a long time to integrate our changes.
It takes a long time to learn the lessons that expand us.
It takes a long time to craft a life of purpose.
It's a life long journey.
Rushing works against us.
Throw out the clocks - the soul has a timeline all its
own.

♡

I used to judge people who didn't want to work on their 'issues' and patterns. I questioned their emotional courage, their fortitude, their depth. To be sure, many of us- myself included- could do a better job of dealing with our stuff head on. But, at the same time, I now recognize that we cannot know how courageous someone else is by looking at their lives from the outside. Perhaps they are carrying around so much unresolved emotional material- their own, even that of the collective- that they do not have any energy left over for processing. Or perhaps they are working in the deep within in ways that we cannot begin to imagine- healing their unresolveds, quietly building the egoic foundation necessary to take on the next level of inner work. It's so hard to know where courage lives.

♡

It is so complicated when the soul is involved, to imagine letting go, but letting go we must, or perhaps, better to think of it as a kind of letting through, letting the pain through the holes it leaves behind so it can find its ultimate destination. With the pain gone, the heart can now open to the next stage on its journey through time(less). Our souls expand when we see each adventure through. All the way through to the transformation at their core. To let go is to let grow...

♡

I am not interested in enlightenment if it means detachment from the emotional body, the earth plane, the challenges of being human. I am interested in Enrealment, because it means that my most spiritual moments are inclusive, arising right in the heart of all that is human: joy and sorrow, shopping list and unity consciousness, fresh mangoes and stale bread. Enrealment is about living in all aspects of reality simultaneously rather than only those realms that feel the most comfortable. We are not just the light, or the mind, or the emptiness, or perpetual positivity. We are the everything. It's ALL God, even the dust that falls off my awakening heart.

♡

Abundance is an odd word. What is abundance to a materialist is not abundance to a spiritual seeker. What is abundance in your mind may not be abundance in your heart. What is abundance to the unhealthy ego may not be abundance to the soul. Best we define our meaning before we ask the universe for more abundance. We might just get it, while the real treasure lies buried below. There is nothing abundant about that which distracts us from a life of meaning. We should be careful what we wish for...

♡

Many of us seek that which we will flee if we find it. I have seen this time and again, both in myself and in others. We seek, we search, and then we find a calling or a relationship that is a perfect reflection of our yearning and we turn away and go back to seeking, almost as though the light of our true-path was too bright for us, too vulnerable for us, too real for us. This is a pattern that we have to recognize and heal or else we will never stop looking for what is already there. True-path is not always around the next corner. Sometimes it's right under our feet.

♡

I consider it a high honor when I am asked to help a fellow human to stay afloat during a difficult time. To be granted the opportunity to gift back to humanity is no small thing. Our sacred purpose often has a relational quality to it. Conceived in union, expressed through union, dying to union with the divine. Always together, never apart. While we are here in embodied form, let's get in close and help each other.

♡

It's a different thing, to make a relationship sacred. When it's just the love you honor, you are still in two different worlds. You love her, she loves you, but what stands between you? What of the bridge between your hearts? What of the world you become together? Conscious relationship is all about the third element- the alchemical combination of two souls merging, the living breathing world that you co-create in love's cosmic kiln. It's the difference between loving and serving love. It's the difference between the narcissistic quest for ecstasy and the joys of deep devotion. You serve loving. You are a devotee to the dance. The conscious-nest is a world unto itself.

♡

I listened intently to the opinions of others about my life's path when I was young. But it didn't help me. No matter how well intentioned their advice was, they couldn't possibly know the true-path I was here to walk. The only place I found my path was deep in my own body-being, a library of wondrous soul-scriptures awaiting my detection and expression.

You are the sculptor of your own reality. Don't hand your tools to anyone else.

♡

Describing a life fueled by callings and sacred purpose only in BIG terms is misleading. Some of us are called to a large, visible canvas, yet that path is no more valuable, or true, or profound than a more subtle path. For many of us, sacred purpose lies in the private places, in the emotional healings, in the shifting patterns, in the warm breezes of transition. It is all sacred purpose, whenever we expand in karmic stature. It is all Go(o)d, whenever we deepen in awareness.

♡

When the student is ready, the student appears.

We're all students, bowing in unison before the great mystery.

♡

When you add soul to sex, it's not sex anymore.
It's God.

♡

You ever notice that when someone communicates something pure and poignant, it is often characterized as something they channeled. It may well be that, but it may also be something they earned at the school of heart knocks. That is, sometimes we come to those places of great clarity through hard, hard work. We clear our debris, we learn our lessons, and then our expression gets crystal clear. I wonder if we call it 'divinely channeled' because we have so much shame as humans that we cannot claim our magnificence. Why must humans channel divinity? After all, we are that, too.

♡

If we have to chase love, it isn't love.
Love meets us halfway.

♡

Those who condemn another's sexual orientation merely reveal the absence of depth in their own sexual lives. Because when you have had the highest form of sexual experience- one that is soul-sourced and soul-driven- you immediately recognize that gender is entirely irrelevant. The soul doesn't care about body parts. It simply loves what it loves.

♡

It's not as simple as changing a tire. You can influence and support others in their transformation, but you can't change them. If there is any learning that I wish had been sealed in my brain at a young age, it is this one. How much time we waste trying to change others, when the only one we can change is staring at us in the mirror.

♡

Just as passive aggressiveness causes suffering, so does passive non-aggressiveness. Passive aggression hurts those who fall victim to its misdirected arrows. Passive non-aggression wounds those who bottle up their expression- their anger congealing into a cache of weapons that explode internally. The healthier approach is to learn how to express anger productively and in a timely manner, so that it doesn't turn outward and harm innocents and so that it doesn't turn inward and cause disease. Because of all the horrible things that humans have done in anger, anger has been given a bad name. But it is a legitimate emotion that signals that we have been violated. It's time we raised healthy anger back to the rafters of acceptability, and work together to clarify a way of expressing it that both holds everyone safe AND allows us to honor its inherent wisdom.

♡

Relationships are like bridges-we can build them up, or knock them down. People often assume that we sever connections because we are carrying a grudge. But that's not always true. Sometimes there is simply no bridge left between the two hearts. We can try to re-build it, but that's not always possible or desired. With our lessons learned, we move on to build a new bridge somewhere else. The hope is that the bridges we form get more stable and nourishing over time.

♡

It was heartbreak that showed me the courage of the feminine. The gift of having your heart smashed open by love and its related disappointments is that you remember what it's like to feel everything again after days, years, lifetimes spent below armor. Through enheartened eyes, we see the courage it takes to stay in the feeling realm. We reward emotional armor because it allows us to 'succeed' in a survivalist world, when we should be honoring those who have the courage to remain emotionally receptive and open on the battlefields of life. It took me this long to realize that remaining heart-centered in this world is the greatest achievement of all.

♡

It's not about living happily ever after. It's about living authentically ever after. Not En'Light'enment, but Enrealment. Embodying a way of being that is genuine, that holds the space for the everything, that can embrace the shadow as it comes, that can see it through to the light-lessons at its heart. Showing up for all of it. Living fully, inclusively, honestly. Living authentically ever after...

♡

You don't measure love in time. You measure love in transformation. Sometimes the longest connections yield very little growth, while the briefest of encounters change everything. The heart doesn't wear a watch- it's timeless. It doesn't care how long you know someone. It doesn't care if you had a 40 year anniversary if there is no juice in the connection. What the heart cares about is resonance. Resonance that opens it, resonance that enlivens it, resonance that calls it home. And when it finds it, the transformation begins...

♡

I always took things personally. If someone looked at me the wrong way, it was about me. If someone rejected me, it was about me. If someone cut me off on the highway, it was about me. This is not unusual for people who grew up in violent, invasive homes. With no boundary to protect us, with so much relational trauma, we cannot distinguish between what is ours, and what is theirs. I remember the first time a therapist said the word 'boundaries' to me. I looked at her puzzled and baffled, unable to grasp this simple concept. And now, after 25 years of healing, I can finally say that I don't take things personally very often. I know where I end, and the other begins. Boundaries, boundaries, boundaries...don't leave home without them.

♡

I considered ending it often when I was a young kid. Poverty, a hateful mother, a violent father, left me feeling so hopeless it was all I could do just to go on. I sat at the precipice of life and death time and again, trying to find a reason to believe. What saved me was a deep belief in something else, a voice inside that told me that it had to be better than that. It was the tiniest little sliver of light. I kept staring at it, holding onto it, praying to it, determined to believe that it was going to grow larger over time. And it did. The little light that knows.

♡

If we age honestly, we become love. As the body weakens, love surges through us, longing to be released, longing to be lived. With no time left to not love, we seek authentic embrace everywhere. Our deft avoidance maneuvers convert into directness. Our armored hearts melt into pools of eternal longing. This is why we should look forward to aging. Finally, after all the masks and disguises fall away, we are left with love alone. God waits for us on the bridge between our hearts.

♡

Yes, it is often a choice we make as to whether we are a victim, or a victor. In many situations, there is a way to look on the bright side, to take responsibility, to focus on the lesson, in our efforts to grow forward. But let's not throw the whole victim out with the bath water. Because sometimes there are victims. Sometimes there are people who did not choose their suffering. Sometimes there are people in such horrifyingly difficult situations that positivity is not enough to save them. And sometimes people actually need to express their victimhood as part of their healing. They need to express it, and they need to be heard. And sometimes they need our help before they can become victors. When we tell them they have a choice, sometimes we forget that WE have a choice too. We can sweep their pain into a swamp of feigned positivity, or we can help them up. We can ignore their challenges or we can support their liberation. Yes, we have a choice, too.

♡

I am all for respecting remarkable people, but there is a fine line between healthy respect and unhealthy adulation. If only we got as excited about saying hello to the stars within us as we do to the stars outside of us, the world would be a much healthier place. So let's give it a try- Ask yourself for your own autograph now and then. Scream with delight when you see yourself in the mirror. Hide behind a tree and take a picture of yourself when you walk out from behind it. Send yourself some fan mail. Fame begins at home.

♡

You can only heal your heart with your heart, and to do that we have to open the heart wide enough for its healing elixir to rain down on our pain. Why bury the tears that heal us? Why bury the emotions that fertilize our expansion? Emotional release is a potent way to regain a genuine experience of the moment. Tears are God's heartshield wipers. They clear the dirt from our heart so we can see the path clearly. Let our quest for spiritual expansion begin with emotional authenticity. Nothing to hide, nowhere to hide it.

♡

It took me many years to realize that everyone involved in the abandonment dance was living out their own stuff- even the warm and connective women who seemed so perfectly available for love. Although they appeared to have a greater capacity for intimacy than I did, the fact that they danced with my unavailability suggested otherwise. They wanted me for the same reasons I wanted the distancers- as a reflection and perpetuation of their unresolved issues. It is no accident that we were all on the same dance floor together- we were all looking for dance partners in an empty ballroom.

♡

This is the thing that many women seldom understand about armored men. They often focus on the fact that the men aren't connecting with them. This is true, and they have every right to feel frustrated by this, but they also need to see the bigger picture. The reality is that many of those men aren't connecting with themselves either. From the beginning, men have been cast in the role of warrior-protector and their emotional armor is fundamental to this task. They are so saturated in their warrior conditioning, so blocked by their emotional holdings, that many of them cannot open their hearts to love's mysteries. It's not that they are consciously withholding intimacy- they simply have no idea how to open to it, and they see perpetual surrender as an unconscious threat to their duty as protector. Vigilance and surrender make strange bedfellows.

♡

We are not just here together to keep each other company. We are here together to show each other God.

♡

I am coming to believe that we commit a great disservice to ourselves when we jump to sexual intimacy before we have established a relational foundation for the connection. Soul-gazing without ground to support it is merely a bliss trip. It's just a matter of time before we come crashing down to earth. The keys to the temple should not be handed out hastily. In-to-me-see needs feet before it can fly. Real connection is a sole to soul proposition.

♡

Normal. Now, there's a word. Healthy. A little better, but still stuck in the same conceptual morass. I prefer Authentic. Yes, that's it. Because it's subjectively defined. You know when you are being authentic. Authentic as the new normal. Authentic as the new healthy. If we start there, we have a chance of creating a healthy normal.

Be real now.

♡

Repressed emotions are unactualized spiritual lessons.

♡

I have had wonderful moments when alone with the Godself in nature, in dance, in music. Like many lone-wolf warriors, I was sure I could go deepest alone, when there was nothing to distract or trigger me. And for a long time I did. But time and hard inner work have shifted my perspective in the direction of personal relationship as my path to God. Not just any relationship, but those that hit you in the soul-ar plexus, that give you new eyes, that reach inside of your heart and soften its edges. They may not end well, but their mission is accomplished as soon as they open you.

♡

We are much too hard on ourselves. Really we are. We beat ourselves up, we 'should' on ourselves, we compare ourselves to others, we postpone self-love until we reach a stage of perfection that is impossibly unrealistic. We are so hard on ourselves, but how are we to know better? It's not like there is a book that lays it all down. It's not like we downloaded perfection. We are still writing that book, writing it with the blood of lessons learned, writing it with ink that is forged in the fires of transformation. We are learning as we g(r)o(w). So let's give ourselves a break. Often. Kindly. Gently. Really. It's a huge thing to grow beyond the parameters of our familiar ways of being. Berating ourselves won't get us anywhere. A little self-love goes a long way…

♡

It's not just the weapons of mass destruction that worry me. It's also the weapons of mass distrAction: unconscious consumerism, self-avoidant behavior, misplaced aggression, substitute gratifications. In fact, if we embody the sacred purpose encoded in the bones of our being, we will lay down our arms and open our hearts to humanity. When the heart is unfettered and alight, the guns drop away. If we stop distracting, we will stop destroying.

♡

Let there be no doubt, love is a sculptor that works you from the inside out. With your heart as its clay, it reaches deep inside you and re-shapes your inner world. One form, then another, then another...

♡

Imagine if we lined up to give our compassion the way we line up to buy stuff.

♡

You are beautifully enough. Your stories of 'not good enough' are fictional novels written by a culture still hiding its light under a mountain of shame. The REAL story, your TRUE autobiography, is one of inherent magnificence, courage and divinity flowing through your soul-veins. So you decide which book to read— the fictional novel written by those who do not SEE you, or the HOLY BOOK written by your glorious spirit.

♡

Suffering in relationship is one path to waking up, but only one path. Sometimes we can grow in the heart of joy. Sometimes we can grow in the heart of peace. Sometimes we can grow in the heart of compassion. If they don't help you glow, then let them go.

♡

I have long been a student of the relationship between chaos and order. When I was younger, my inner world was emotionally chaotic and unresolved. In an effort to create a measure of balance, I was obsessed with external order- a perfectly clean house, a straightly hung picture, everything in its place. But it never quite worked- just when I got one thing 'perfect,' I was looking for the next thing to perfect. And then I turned my attention to the real issue- my inner chaos. Interestingly, the more work I did to clear my emotional debris, the less I cared about having everything perfect on the outside. The balance had shifted. This is my way of saying that what matters most is inner peace. Through that lens, the dust of the world is of little consequence.

♡

The poor EGO. The heavy booted bypassers just keep crushing it under foot, without giving it any credit at all. The poor EMOTIONAL BODY. They keep crushing it under foot, without giving it any credit at all. The poor BODY TEMPLE. They keep crushing it under foot, without giving it any credit at all. The poor PERSONAL IDENTITY. They keep crushing it under foot, without giving it any credit at all. The poor DUALITY. They keep crushing it under foot, without giving it any credit at all. Not much left after all that crushing. Might have to send in a retrieval squad to make us whole again. Where do they think spirituality lives, if not in the heart of our HUMANNESS? Enrealment demands that all of our aspects have a seat at the table.

♡

Ignore everything that doesn't serve the honoring of your purpose. Not ignore as in deny reality- ignore as in find a way to keep your eyes on the purpose at the end of the tunnel no matter what is pressing up against you. We lose our way when we get so lost in our distractions that we wander from our path. But when we can hold a vision of purpose safe no matter what...it deepens within us and ensures that we will honor it when the moment is right.

♡

If we teach the young ones sacred purpose as path, they won't confuse substitute gratifications with a life of meaning.

♡

I used to ask my therapist, "When will I be done with all this hard work so my real life can begin?" She would laugh and say "This IS your real life." I wasn't pleased. But now I get it- my challenges and issues were the grist for the soul-mill, the interpretive field for my soul's expansion. To the extent that I could work them through, I matured in my spirituality and lived more fully. To the extent that I bypassed them, I remained stuck and confused. It's not to say that we don't want more pleasure in our lives -we surely do- but there is also something to be said for honoring our shadow and inviting it into consciousness as a friend bearing gifts: "Hello, old friend, come on in, we have work to do..."

♡

Truth is the gateway to the moment.

♡

Sometimes we forget how far we have traveled while we are looking ahead to the next steps. Good to lie down and remember what it took to get this far, all those karmic hoops we had to jump through, all those overcomings. Good to stroke our face with love and to remind ourselves how much courage it took and who we would have become if we hadn't braved the journey. Good to say 'thank you' to the inner spirit that walks within and beside us, whispering sweet somethings in our inner ear, reminding us that we are simply and utterly worth fighting for. We ARE simply and utterly worth fighting for.

♡

Sometimes love finds you when it's ready. And when you're ready too. How that happens is anybody's guess. Love is the great mystery stew, its secrets well kept, its ingredients known to providence alone. While both people are being prepared, marinated, skewered, cooked to readiness in the fires of life, the cosmic alchemist is turning the pot, reverently preparing the base for the lovers who will meld into it. Only God knows when the stew is ready to be served. Divine timing, Divine dining…

♡

The wonderful thing about this life, for those of us who are able to stick around, is that we get so many opportunities to come back into reality, even if we had to numb ourselves to stay alive, even if we disconnected for a very long time. I love how God set it up so that the path rises up to meet us time and again, inviting us to set our feet back on our own unique true-path yet another time. This is the nature of karmic gravity—we are returned back to our path until we fully walk it. Return to sender, address now known...

♡

If real love reveals anything, it is that finding your soul-mate does not mean finding perpetual bliss. If it does, then it is love flying at half-mast. If a love is that deep, it is a portal to the everything, shredding through the adaptations and disguises that disconnect us from reality, excavating shadow and light from their hiding places. The glory and the gory rise into awareness in unison, calling us to the sky and the earth in one fell swoop. Real soulmates are actually wholemates, penetrating the everything on the wings of their love.

♡

I often try to imagine a world where we are not in competition with our fellow humans, but where we truly, madly, deeply soulebrate when others actualize their dreams. Imagine that. A world where we get excited for each other when we achieve- where we do not see another's accomplishments as a reminder of what we have not yet actualized- but as living proof that it is possible for all of us. I love it when people accomplish something they have set out to do, when the phoenix rises from the ashes with actualization on its wings. Let's invite each other higher. Let's encourage each other to believe in our shared magnificence!

♡

Although meditation was a helpful spiritual practice, it also reminded me of the limits of solo travel. When I would expand my consciousness in isolation, on the meditation cushion, alone in nature, at the tail end of an emotional release, there was a way in which I could never touch eternity. It was like I was skirting the edges of God- touching her toes, smelling her skin, watching her breathe- without ever penetrating her depths. With love as my meditation, God opened herself completely to me, inviting me deeper in with every breath stroke. In loving my beloved, in surrendering to the merger along the heart-genital highway, another portal opened, one where the eternal nature of soul-life was revealed. Our unified soul was the alchemical combination that showed us God.

♡

I love to see dear friends assert necessary boundaries in celebration of their own value. There is something so in-powering, so transformative, so forward-moving about standing our ground in situations where we have been habitually stuck. We send a message to the deep within that we truly matter. That message melts our shame and liberates us on many unseen levels, preparing us for the next stage of our self-creation journey.

♡

I used to believe that the only way I could change was if I had a peak experience, or a nervous breakthrough, or won a noisy battle with a relentless pattern. This emphasis on dramatic transition was a reflection of my dramatic early life, one where nothing ever seemed to happen subtly. But I was wrong. Some transitions do have to happen in the heart of intensity, but not all do. In fact, many cannot happen that way- the drama just intensifies the armor that surrounds the pattern. Instead, some patterns transform slowly, carefully, subtly over time. We unravel one thread, then another, then another, until the structure melts into the next way of being on our path. So much happens in the quiet within. So much.

♡

Perhaps this is why it's so very difficult to lose a soul-mate. You don't just lose your companion. You don't just lose your friend. You don't just lose your lover. You lose your portal to divinity. You lose your gateway to God. You lose the whole bloody universe.

And then you find it again. In your heartbreak. In your healing. In the learning of the lesson that expands you. In the strengthening and re-birth of your willingness. In the re-opening to the possibility of love.

Every path is a path to God. We just have to remember to open our hearts again, and again...

♡

I used to try to punch my way through people's walls. I didn't understand that they were there for a reason and often essential to their survival. I did the same with my own walls. Neither got me anywhere. The walls just got tougher, denser, more resilient. Now I have a different approach. I pray to walls. I honor their wisdom. I stroke them with kindness. I melt them with gentleness. And, if they still insist on standing firm, I leave them be. Walls have a timeline all their own.

♡

The trick with manifestation is not to talk about it, but to do it. You can tell everyone your plan, you can ask the universe to support you, you can even hold a special fire ceremony to usher it into realization, but it won't mean anything if you don't ground it in reality. If you are having trouble manifesting, look honestly and lovingly at what may be in the way- unresolved emotional issues, shame and self-doubt, preliminary practical steps. Don't sit and spin- work genuinely on what is blocking the path. And, then, when you are ready, channel that energy into constructive action. If you have a dream- DO IT into being.

♡

So many of us know the moment when a love connection is over, but few of us stop then. I am not talking about reactive endings. I am talking about the deep intuitive knowing that it is time to move on. Yet we are either too afraid, or too stubborn, or too concerned about the other's feelings to make our move. But it is perilous to delay, both because we suffer in the wrong connection, and because we hold two souls back from finding the next step on their individual paths. Whether there is another love waiting around the next corner, or whether it is simply time to be alone, no one benefits by staying in an outgrown union. We have to notice the moment of ending and take it to heart. Everyone's expansion depends on it.

♡

We are human beings having a spiritual experience. And we are spiritual beings having a human experience. And they are exactly the same.

♡

However love arrives at your door, it is always a brave path. It is like taking a long walk in a deep dark forest and never quite knowing where your soul will land. It is not for the faint of heart, nor is it ever to be taken lightly. Real love is heartcore. You have to be tenacious. You have to be innovative. You have to be willing to drop to your knees time and again before its wisdom. And you have to forge the tools you will need from your own imaginings, as very few who have walked the path before can describe the terrain. Most fell into quicksand soon after the romantic phase ended. Relationship is always a spiritual practice, even when we imagine it otherwise.

♡

The price we pay for walking a false-path is tangible. When we hide our true purpose under a mountain of fear, we suffer for it in the form of truth-aches, depression and hopelessness, addictive and self-distractive behavior. The price is high. The price we pay for walking our true-path is also tangible: truth chills, an enlivened emotional body, authenticity as a buffer against the madness of the world. When we excavate our soul-scriptures from their hiding places, we begin to walk in our own shoes. The path is not always easy, but we always know which way we are headed.

♡

This wondrous world doesn't owe me anything. It has given me the gift of breath, eyes, heart, truth, love. It has given me one opportunity after another to awaken and expand. It has shone its light upon me time and again, inviting me to seize the day if I dare. It has picked me up when I have fallen and it has given me new eyes when I have gone blind. It has reminded me of the gift of life every day, in so many seen and unseen ways. If I have not noticed, I have no one else to blame. This wondrous world doesn't owe me anything.

♡

I totally understand that sometimes people did their very best, given their issues and circumstances, even when very bad things happened. But I have a problem when "I did my best" becomes a basis for re-connection, as though that alone is enough. Sometimes we do our very best, but we have to accept that certain relationships cannot be revived. It took me a long time to recognize that I could understand and even forgive certain actions, without choosing to re-connect.

♡

Those who can't embrace their shadow can't embrace their light. It's all, or it's nothing at all.

♡

So much life force is imprisoned below our shackles of shame. Don't listen to the wardens. They are imprisoned, too. Free yourself. You are the only one who can. Open your inner gifts. Hide no light under a bushel. Know that you are here for a reason. Honor your magnificence. When we realize what a treasure we are, it all changes. It really does. Treasure yourself.

♡

I look forward to the day when we can meet one another in our true nakedness, stripped free of unresolved emotions, pain-induced projections, the distortions of duality. For too long we have been on opposite sides of the river, the bridge between our hearts washed away by a flood of pain. But the time has come to construct a new bridge, one that comes into being with each step we take, one that is fortified with benevolent intentions and authentic self-revealing. As we walk toward one another, our emotional armor falls to the ground, transforming into the light at its source. And when we are ready, we walk right into the Godself at the center of the bridge, puzzled that we ever imagined ourselves separate.

♡

It's all very complicated until time makes it simple.

♡

Those who judge others based on their skin color have lost touch with their own souls. The soul cares nothing about race. It has no interest in arbitrary distinctions. It has no interest in the form our earth-suit takes. Through the eyes of essence, we see only essence. Through soulful eyes, race is revealed as just another form on the path to wholeness. But it's not the heart of the matter. Our shared divinity is. We are not here together to shame each other into oblivion. We are here together to show each other God. And God comes in every possible color and form.

♡

Most of the greatest achievements on the planet
are unknown to others- private overcomings, silent
attempts at belief, re-opening a shattered heart.
The real path of champions truly lies within- the
transforming of suffering into expansion, the clearing
of horrifying debris, the building of a healthy self-
concept without tools. The greatest achievers have
found a way to believe in something good despite
being traumatized and fractured on life's battlefields.
No matter what else they accomplish in their lives,
they are already champions. One day the world will
realize that it is much harder to heal a shattered heart
than excel at athletics. Go(l)d medals all around...

♡

It is amazing how certain soul connections can deepen our experience of the moment, even in their (seeming) absence. The energy of the connection opens doors where before there were none, portals to the great within and the great beyond. I appreciate the great waves of unity consciousness that can emerge when alone with God, but somehow imagine that the ultimate experience of wholeness comes through connection- love as gateway, love as rehearter, love as a reflection of all that is possible. Certain connections paint pictures of possibility in the sky, expanding our lens for all eternity.

♡

I think of my father's passing and I think of how narrowly we define success. The culture sets the bar unnaturally, imagining success in linear, objective, externalized terms. You are a success if you make a fortune, or become famous, or win awards. No, no, success is actually something else, something more subtle and incremental, something internally true and privately held. I think of my father's traumatic life and recognize what a profound success it was for him to simply stay alive, to shift his lens toward positivity, to smooth the rough edges forged in life's fires. That alone was extraordinary. Success is finding a way to grow in the heart of a hopeless landscape. To that I bow.

♡

We are powerful beyond measure, and so deeply vulnerable at the same time. This may seem like a dichotomy, but it isn't. We have misunderstood real power. It has been something assertive, non-surrendering, pushing on through. This is not real power. This is simply willfulness. Real power is something else—receptivity, vulnerability, the courage to keep your heart open on the darkest of days, the strength to feel it all even when the odds are stacked against you. Real power is showing up with your heart on your sleeve and absolutely refusing to waste one moment of your life hidden behind edginess and armor. The art of enheartened presence. Now that's power.

♡

A great door opens every time we walk our own way. Not the way of the world, not the way of the other, but the way that is encoded in the bones of our being. It is not easy to open the great door in an inauthentic world, but open it we must. On the other side of the door, our real life awaits. Walk with your head high and your heart open. The universe responds to authentic transformation. Nothing false will do.

♡

The armored man is afraid of his heart, he is afraid of the empowered feminine, he is afraid of surrendering his egoic shield to something deeper, truer, more heartfelt. What he doesn't realize is that we are inextricably linked, so linked that when he denigrates the feminine, he imprisons and denigrates his own consciousness. There can be no victories at the expense of the Divine Mother. None at all. It is time for a new paradigm, one that honors the wisdom of the feminine, one that soulebrates her courageous willingness to remain receptive, relational, and compassionate in the heart of this still mad world. Armored men- bow before her. Sing her praises, dance in her wisdom and her love. She is the path home.

♡

It's often difficult to distinguish a soul-mate from a wound-mate because powerful connections excavate the unresolved emotional material that each of us holds. The stronger the connection, the stronger the light shining on those dark places. Some wound-mates truly do contain the seeds of our soulular expansion. But not all wound-mates are soul-mates. Sometimes they are toxic connections masquerading as something more heightened. Sometimes they are destructive battle-grounds with very little possibility for expansion. Sometimes they are just trouble with a capital T. It's an important distinction. We want to go where we grow.

♡

I love the path of service and try not to lose sight of the fact that I am doing it for me. It's not an unselfish act of giving. Whenever I give anything to another, they are also giving to me. By receiving my gift, they are gifting me back. They are allowing me to honor my own calling to service. Our Soulshaping is always reciprocal in nature. We grow together...

♡

Every time we don't stand down the primary abusers in our lives, we lose a little ground, we fade into the night, we die a little inside. Rising above it may be a temporary balm, but, at some point, we have to come back into our bodies and speak it. As important as it is to reach a stage of genuine forgiveness where possible, it is even more important to assert boundaries with those who have violated ours. It may well be why they came into our lives- to force us to recognize and claim our own value.

♡

I imagine each of us a safe-cracker, except that the safe lives within us. Everywhere we look for signs- in our dreamscapes, in our truth-aches, in our longing for purpose- in our earnest efforts to crack our own karmic code. There's a buried treasure at the heart of this incarnation, we just know it. Deep within us are the soul-scriptures that we are here to excavate, to liberate, to humanifest. A conscious life is one where our inner ear is always close to the lock, listening in for the just-right combination that will open us wide. And when it does, life takes on a whole new meaning, infused with the light of our unique sacred purpose. What a treasure we are.

♡

When you have loved as God loves, you no longer yearn for companionship in the same way. You no longer feel isolated when you walk alone. Because you have been penetrated by divinity. Because you have been transformed beyond yourself. Because you walk in shared shoes. Because you always feel the beloved close at heart.

♡

If you get God, you get Goddess.
Can't have one without the (M)other.

♡

Our security blanket is often what suffocates us. It's one thing if what secures us is congruent with our sacred purpose, but if it isn't, then what have we gained? The illusion of security at the expense of our authenticity. Better we prioritize our truest path above all else. Better we trust our soul's calling. Then we can sleep without a security blanket, warmed by the fires of our authenticity. Better to live true.

♡

Detachment may be a necessary survival tool for a time, but sustainable growth demands that we come back down to earth and work with what lives inside of us. Bypass models are merely tools, defenses and coping strategies. They are short term way stations on the path to wholeness. In fact, the very idea that we are seeking a 'heightened consciousness' is a direct reflection of a bypassing lens. Our expansion is not waiting for us in the sky- we aren't birds- it's waiting within us, where Reality Road meets Inclusivity Lane, in the Village of Wholeness. At the end of the day, you don't rise above anything. You live it through the bones of your being. Who needs higher, when we are already living right inside the God temple? Walk walk walkin' on heaven's floor.

♡

Love is just a concept until it's real…
And then it makes no sense at all.

♡

Everybody has their issues. It's what we do with them that determines our life. Not to dwell on our issues, not to pretend they aren't real, but to do all we can to work them through to the transformation at their core. There's gold in them there spills...

♡

If one person doesn't want the relationship, then it's simply not a fit. No sense trying to figure out why we think they don't want it. No sense blaming it on their commitment issues. No sense waiting around for them to realize they wanted it after all. Because it doesn't matter why they don't want it. What matters is that we want to be met heart-on by a fully engaged partner. If they don't want it, then we don't want it, because we don't want to be with someone who is not there for it fully. That's the thing about love relationship- it's an agreement that has to be signed by both souls. If one doesn't sign, then nothing has been lost. If it's not a fit for them, it's not a fit for us either. On to the next adventure we go..

♡

I refuse to soul-out. If the opportunities presented to me are not congruent with my true path- no matter how egoically or economically gratifying they may be- the answer is simply NO. At the end of the day, I have to live with the authenticity of my choices. Nothing matters more.

♡

One of the greatest measures of the work I have done to solidify my sense of self is how I respond to disappointment in my relationships with others. If I close my heart in response, then I know I am still inclined to give too much power away. If I keep my heart open, then I know that I am moving from a solid sense of self. Through the eyes of a healthy self-concept, no one is granted the right to close my heart, no matter how horrifying their behavior, no matter how disappointing the outcome. Now, after many years of handing it over, the final key always remains with me.

♡

May we never forget the relational and co-transformative nature of human expansion. Although the ultimate romance is with your own soul, it is our experiences together that give birth to the essential lessons. We are each here to participate in this dance of sacred imagination, stepping on each other's toes and turning each other toward God one clumsy step after another. We trip, and then we get back up with greater awareness. With this in heart, I am hopeful that we can learn to accept one another in our humanness. We are going to continue to make mistakes, but there is grace in that if we see our errors through to the lessons they contain.

♡

Unresolved pain can bury us so deep in the ground that we can't see beyond it, or it can act like a trampoline, bouncing us away from reality in an effort to bypass it. Either way, we are doomed until we make a conscious decision to work our stuff all the way through to completion. That decision changes everything, offering us a golden opportunity to transform our consciousness and embrace the light. I think of how much changed when I decided to stop blaming the world and simply own my stuff. New eyes.

♡

That we are here means we are blessed. No need to look for your blessings out there. They live at the heart of every breath. If we are here, we are wanted here. If we are here, we have a role to play. If we are here, we have a place in this madhouse of delights. That we are here means we are blessed.

♡

It's never rude to interrupt your false self. I just asked mine to give it a rest. I think he was relieved. So much hard work for so little reward. Sleep my masked friend, sleep.

♡

I practice the art of NND (No Needless Dramas) whenever possible. Before, I loved drama- it was a perpetuation of my childhood home- and I mistook intensity for life itself. But there is a huge difference between intensity and aliveness. Looking back, I truly don't know how I got anything done in my high-intensity lifestyle. Most of my energy went to putting out fires... fires I had started! At first, it was uncomfortable to let this go, as the calm brought up all kinds of unresolved feelings- but it became more comfortable over time. With NND as my earnest companion, I am now able to focus on my sacred purpose without getting in my own way. You would be amazed how much energy we have for life when we say farewell to needless dramas.

♡

Eat your stuff, before your stuff eats you.

♡

That's the thing about great love. It elevates everything around it. You walk through a forest together and it becomes a great temple. You eat a meal together and you sit at God's banquet table. You merge your bodies and all heaven breaks loose. That's why we can't stop singing about love. Every verse is a serenade into wholeness.

♡

I love humanity. Even though we are so bloody mixed up, so blind to our wondrous nature, so afraid of the love that sources our existence, I can't stop believing in us. The way we overcome, the way we find the faith, the way we craft light in the darkest of tunnels, is just the tip of the soulberg. There is something beautiful waiting for us, a poetic magnificence, a wellspring of genie-us that will not die until humanity embodies it fully. When we are ready, the rivers of essence will rise up to meet us and we will know the glory of this human form. I just can't stop believing in this humanity. I won't.

♡

Love is all there is. All else, disguises.

♡

Because of all the pressure to be partnered, so many people walk around feeling badly if they are on their own, and many others stay where they don't belong for fear that they will be seen as a failure outside of relationship. Surely all of this misses the point. What is most important is that each of us lives a life that is true to path, whatever that means to us. For some, their sacred purpose is inextricably linked to love relationship. It is there that they excavate and humanifest their deepest meaning. Yet others are called in a different direction and find their purpose in their creative life, in their work, in their individual spiritual practice. Everyone's soul-scriptures are unique to their own journey. The important thing in life is not whether we find the "one", but whether we find the path.

Peace with path. It's that simple. Peace with path.

♡

This life is a hero's journey. Anyone who sticks it out and gives it their best shot is heroic, in my eyes. What we call normal is so often extraordinary. Just overcoming the weight of the world, and making a genuine effort to identify and honor our true-path is profound. Kudos to anyone who is making a genuine effort to get through this life with originality, awareness and authenticity.

♡

It's not about giving up on the fairy tale relationship. It's about landing it in reality. It's about giving the fairy feet. It's about peeling away the prince's armor and loving the human down below. It's about wiping off the princess' make-up and loving her divine humanness. It's about finding romance in the naked fires of daily life. When our masks and disguises fall away, real love can reveal itself. Forget fairy tales- the human tale is much more satisfying. We just have to learn how to get turned on by humanness.

♡

That's the expansive nature of a great love experience between two souls. The deeper they go, the less it is about them and the more it is about the collective. With their love as rocket-fuel, they are catapulted right into the heart of divine. There they become one with all that is- the light and the shadow, the healed and the unresolved, the glory and the gory. They become more than two branches of the human tree- they become the entire forest. This is why traditional psychotherapy often fails soul-mates. Early childhood issues don't even begin to cover the vast array of triggers that come up when souls merge with the divine. What we actually need are Love Elders, those who have ridden love's highways into eternity. We need to commune with those who have been there before us.

♡

It doesn't change when we stare at it from across the room. It doesn't change when we sit in prayer and wish it away. It doesn't change when we skirt the edges of the shadow. It doesn't change when we pretend it's all Go(o)d. It changes when we cross the sacred battleground willing to die to our truth. It changes when we look the lie in the eye until it has nowhere left to hide. It changes when we pick up the sword of truth and cut the falsity until it bleeds. The era of the sacred activist is upon us. Not the warrior run amok, but the benevolent warrior who fights for our right to the light. Some battles are worth fighting.

♡

I am all for meditation and other peaceful approaches to deepen our experience of the moment. But I am also a firm advocate for embodied enlivened emotional release work as well. All too often, we associate spirituality with something peaceful, but that's too limiting a definition. Spirituality actually means reality. The more spiritual person explores and embodies all realms and experiences. That includes the unresolved emotional body - which does not go away when we witness it ('the Witness Bypass') - but which needs to be moved through with heartfelt determination. Releasing the tears and anger fully creates space inside for new experiences to enter and actually brings us more peacefully into the moment. How to know the now if our consciousness is still back in the then? With the past expressed and resolved, we can actually experience the moment with genuine presence.

♡

There is a time to seek, and a time to find. Seeking, exploring, excavating our true path is essential to the journey, but we need to be careful not to miss the signs that we have discovered something that is ready to be lived. Sometimes we know more than we are admitting to ourselves about our path because we are afraid to live our truth fully. Perhaps we were not met with acceptance and support when we revealed who we were; perhaps we are afraid of the consequences of owning our path. Whatever stands in the way, let us courageously live what we find so that we can expand into wholeness. The universe delights in our actualization.

♡

If there is anything that can prevent us from excavating and honoring our callings, it is our own shame. With our light hidden beneath layers of shame, it is very difficult to imagine our highest possibilities. If we think we are worthless, how can we spot the God-self that lives inside of us? How can we know our inherent magnificence? Your shame has nothing to say about who you really are. It never did, never will. In truth, you don't need anyone else's permission to be here. God gave you all the permission you need.

♡

I think of the river when I think of emotional processes. When it dams, it dies. It needs to keep moving to stay alive. Humans are the same. Depression is frozen feeling. When we dam up our emotions, we die. We need to keep the river of feeling moving. Our life, and our presence, depend on it.

♡

One of my most treasured learnings has been that of appreciation, particularly for special friendships when they come. When we are young, we often think everything will happen again. We have the arrogance of youth, imagining opportunities will always repeat themselves. But some wonderful things only happen once. We need to take better care of our blessings.

♡

I am all for aha! moments and other peak experiences, but my most lasting transformation happened in the subtleties, in those private moments of decision as to which path to walk. In every moment, there is a choice: Will I open, or close? Will I take responsibility, or blame? Will I download the learning, or deflect? Will I go to my edge, or fall back to safety? Will I honor my intuition, or listen to the world? Millions of moments of decision that inform who we become. Getting out of Unconscious Prison is a life-long journey. True path is built with choices. I choose authenticity.

♡

I strongly dislike when people try to hold people back from actualizing their wholeness. That's where we have been, but it isn't where we are going. We must stand firmly against lite-dimmers and invite in only those who rejoice in our successes. That's the real soulpod- those who stand around us cheering us on every time we take a step toward embodying our inherent magnificence. Those who can delight in our achievements. Those who can love us without agenda. Those who recognize that humanity cannot move forward until we are all thrilled by each other's successes.

I wish for you everything that makes you whole.

♡

There is the now, and there is the NOW. Not talking about the now that removes our emotional body, our ego, our personal identifications and unresolved feelings from the moment. Not talking about the now that is self-avoidance masquerading as enlightenment. Talking about the now that includes everything human in the experiential equation, that honors the self instead of bypassing it, that doesn't look for its purpose in the emptiness but in the heart of the self, it-self. You want to live in the now? Don't transcend this human form- Include it. Embody it. Enliven it. Now.

♡

Heart is the new hot.

♡

Everyone decides what love is for them. Some of us stop at practicality. And some of us will only stop when the most profound love connection walks through the door. The practical ones have a much better chance of lasting. But the soulful ones actually have a chance to touch God. Their odds are lower, but they don't much care. Better an occasional banquet with God than 3 meals a day with a stranger. Pick your path...

♡

The culture pushes young people too hard to define who they are before they have lived enough to know. How can they know such things? It makes sense that we want them to have a focus so they can meet their own needs, but how to clarify true-path, how to individuate from cultural and parental messaging, how to excavate their callings, before they have gone out into the world and gathered information from their experiences. No wonder there are so many identity crises in middle age- we defined ourselves from the outside in when we were young! It may seem counter-intuitive in a pragmatic, survivalist culture, but the young need to be encouraged to embrace and explore their confusion wholeheartedly. In the heart of the not knowing are the paths they are here to walk.

♡

There are two types of relational silence- one that serves the connection, one that damages it. In the first, silence comes with the qualifier "I need some quiet time to reflect", which is healthy and respectful to the connection. In the second, silence comes with no qualifier and others are left to wonder what is actually happening. In this case, silence is actually violence- a passive aggressive attempt to cause suffering, or, at the least, a negligent self-absorption that makes things worse. Given that so many of us grew up with the silent treatment, it is essential that we let others know what is happening when we go quiet. It is respectful and it keeps the love alive. Even something like "Time out!" can be enough to keep silence from turning into violence.

♡

There is a path at the heart of each love connection. Each has its own karmic blueprint. It is seldom what we imagine. You just have to find the path and follow it wherever it leads you. Some connections are meant to last a lifetime, and many aren't. Expectations are like quicksand. They keep us from arriving at our true destination. Love is the great expander. Wherever we land, may we arrive with our hearts stretched open. Painful, maybe, but one stretch closer to wholeness.

♡

I cannot help but marvel at the human capacity to overcome tremendous suffering and find a way to go on. It would be one thing if we released all our holdings right after the trauma, but that we continue to carry them and still find the faith to believe in a better tomorrow is simply heroic. I think of the shadow material that takes up space inside many of us- repressed emotions, unsaid words, armored musculature, collective trauma- and then marvel at our capacity to weave optimism, faith and determination into the heart of it. Minefields and goldmines sitting side by side in the inner valley. Let's stop looking for our heroes 'out there.' They are staring at us in the mirror.

♡

I didn't realize how alone I was, until I wasn't. It is such a relief when great love comes your way after years, lifetimes without it. Let there be no doubt that all love connections are not created equal. Some bonds are simply practical. Others are blindly rooted in pathology and old traumas. Still others are opportunities to heal and have essential needs finally met. And some have a mystical quality from the first meeting. Pure and simple. Apparent from the first out-breath. Unmistakably sacred. God rising on the wings of their love. This is how the timely and the timeless become indistinguishable- when love meets God deep in the heart's inner temple.

♡

Exchange your righteousness
for humanness,
your judgments for compassion,
your hopelessness for faith,
your armor for love.

Such a sweet planet we live on
when we walk it with heart.

♡

May we always find a sliver of light when we need it most. May we support each other in shamelessly sharing our inner worlds so that no one suffers alone. And may we give each other a little bit of our own light when we have some to spare. Surely there is enough light to go around.

♡

Love it Forward.

♡

You are Sacred Purpose

You are Sacred Purpose.

You are not your shame, your fears, your addictions, your games, your guilt, the internalized remnants of negative messaging. You are not your resistance to your true path. You are not your self-doubt. You are not your self-distraction patterns. You are not your escape hatches. You are not your pessimism about a life of meaning and purpose. You are not here merely to survive and endure.

You are Sacred purpose.

No matter what others have mistakenly told you about who you are, no matter what mistakes you may have made in the past, you are here with a sacred purpose living at the core of your being. If that weren't true you never would have made it down the birth canal. You never would have overcome what you have already overcome in your life. You would not be here at all.

You are Sacred Purpose.

Whatever your ways of distracting, postponing, delaying, armoring, avoiding, altering, feigning, artificializing, externalizing, superficializing your life... I encourage you to STOP IT NOW. This really is no game, this is completely real; this sacred purpose that courses through your soul veins crying out to be heard from below the surface of your avoidance. I cannot say this with enough assertiveness... To the extent that you identify and honor your true path in this lifetime, you will know genuine satisfaction, real peace in your skin. You will be infused with vitality and a clarified focus, new pathways of possibility appear where before there were obstacles. You will know a peace that will buffer you against the madness of the world, a clarity of direction that will carry you from one satisfaction to another. Life will still have its challenges, but you will interface with them differently, coated in an authenticity of purpose that sees through the veils to what really matters. To the extent that you avoid the quest for purpose, you will live frustrated, a half-life... your avoidance manifest in all manner of illness, perpetual dissatisfaction, emotional problems, depression, addictive patterns, all reflections of your own alienation from the purposeful root of your being. You see, there really is no escape from reality. There is only postponement. You should be more afraid of avoiding your path than walking it.

You are Sacred Purpose.

AND- it doesn't matter what anyone tells you about who you are. There is so much of that. This is your journey. Even those with the best of intentions, cannot know the path you are here to walk. The REAL journey is not one of adapting yourself to someone else's vision, but, instead, shaping who you are with your own two hands. The unique clay you work with lives deep inside your soul bones, awaiting your own detection and expression. You are the sculptor of your own reality- don't hand your tools to anyone else. Only you can know the path you are here to walk. It's a personal decision, and it doesn't have to be grandiose. Your purpose can be as simple as learning how to listen better, how to enjoy the moment without getting in your own way... wherever the growing is, wherever you find genuine peace with path, wherever you feel unmasked and genuinely real.

In the survivalist world that we are coming from, we defined ourselves by what got us through the day, whatever masks got food on the table, whatever way of being endured this challenging life. But we are at the beginning of a new way, a way of being that is sourced in who we REALLY ARE, not our egoic face, not our survivalist face, not the false face of our hidden power, but the real face, the real path, the no bullshit no hype no pretense expression of WHO YOU REALLY ARE and a life that fully and deeply expresses the magnificence that lives within you. Your sacred purpose may be covered in dust, it may be hidden from view, but it's still in there, sparkling with infinite possibility. There is a sacred purpose alive in each of us, a chaotic magnificence of epic proportions, a fire that will not die until it burns through our doubt and our shame and lights our way home.

You are Sacred Purpose.

This is a call to action. A call to authenticity. A call to dig yourself out from below the bushel of shame and self-doubt that has plagued humanity. A call to get off the dime and do the real work to admit your distraction patterns and excavate your purpose in this lifetime. What are you here to learn? What are you here to overcome? What are you here to express? What does your authentic face look like? Who are you, above and beyond all the noise and haste? This is not about money, or bullshit ideas of abundance, or gratifying your ego. This is about the real thing, the real deal, the vulnerable and courageous truth about who you are and why you are here. I encourage you to take the question of sacred purpose seriously... to not postpone it for another hour, or week, or until you retire, until the next lifetime, until you finish school, or end your relationship. I encourage you to take it seriously NOW... To work like a dog to feverishly unbury what lives inside of you, what you are here to express, what you are here to manifest, what you are here to give, to share, to learn, to create, to dance, to art, to walk.... You don't know how long you have, it may be 60 years, it may be 60 seconds, you may not make it to retirement, you may not make it to tomorrow morning. If you are questing for your purpose, if you are living your truth, you will not suffer when it is time to leave your body in this lifetime. You will be living in your authenticity- this is no small achievement in this distracted world, where the unconscious media and manipulative marketers try to make us generic and frightened so we will be locked into their script... f^#k that. You already have a script and it lives deep inside you. That script is your purpose, what you are here to express, to learn, to embody, to humanifest. So you decide which script to read- the fictional novel written by those who do not SEE you, or the HOLY BOOK written by your glorious spirit. When you walk through the gateway of purpose, you walk into yourself.

You are sacred purpose, you are sacred purpose, you are sacred purpose.

Don't stop until you find it.

J.B., 2011
(originally published on Vivid Life
(www.vividlife.me) on Dec. 27, 2011)

Drinking from an Empty Glass: A Letter to a Dear, Dark Friend

Yes, I know the government is corrupt. Yes, I know there are people conspiring. Yes, I know people can lack integrity. Yes, I know that western culture is materialistic. Yes, I know that corporations are self-serving. Yes, I know that the media is manipulative. Yes, I know it is hard to trust love. Yes, I know that it can be difficult to believe in God. I share many of your concerns.

And I also know that we cannot change the world without acknowledging what is wrong. I know that we must stand against that which shames, oppresses and damages humanity. I know that we should not ignore the injustices and put on a fake smile. I know that we must find our voice and stand our ground. I know that we must fight for our right to the light. I believe deeply in forward moving criticism.

But something doesn't feel quite right. You complain all the time. You have made negativity a full time job. You don't make an effort to find solutions. You blame everything on the world out there. You don't actually do anything positive to effect change. And you seldom acknowledge the positive steps humanity has made. You seldom acknowledge the beauty around you. You almost never see the light in the darkness.

I know something from my lived experience. I know that the light is always there. It is there, in the breath that keeps you alive, in the smile of a child, in the yet another chance to find your path. It is there in the rise of the feminine, in the therapeutic revolution, in the burgeoning quest for authenticity. If you can't see it, then the issue is a personal one, for there are signs of progress everywhere.

And I also know from a lifetime of overcoming that it is possible to hold it all at once. To fight against injustice while still embodying the light. To see where we are lacking, while rejoicing in our abundance. To express our anger, and to live our gratitude. To feel overwhelmed by an unfair world, while still achieving our goals. To see how far we have yet to travel, while applauding how far we have come.

And so I wonder what lives below your perpetual negativity? Apart from the problems with the world, what happened that darkened your lens? What made the glass so empty? Is it really all about the world 'out there', or are there also unresolved personal experiences that need to be healed? What are you really trying to express about the lack of love, attention, and satisfaction in your life? What lives below this victimhood? What is your deeper complaint? What needs to expressed and resolved so that you will see some light shining through again? Please don't wait until the world is perfect, for it will never be so.

Dear friend, how can I help you to believe again?

J.B., 2013
*(originally published on Vivid Life
(www.vividlife.me) on July 9, 2013)*

Apologies to my (Sweet) Body
(from a head-tripper in transition)

I apologize for hiding from you in my mind. I was a head-tripper extraordinaire, preferring the seeming safety of my thoughts to the often savage world of feeling. Although I was frequently called 'absent-minded', I was actually 'absent-bodied', living far outside the walls of the body temple. I grew up in a hateful family, and feeling into my body meant feeling into the horrible memories held in my tissues. Surviving by my wits allowed me to think my way through challenging circumstances and shielded me from pain. But my headiness came at a price- excessive analysis perpetuates emotional paralysis. My coping strategy became my blueprint for reality, alienating me from my real life. But I want to stop watching you from afar. I want to open the gate and come back in now.

I apologize for abusing you with toxic food, overeating, workaholism. I wanted you drained and deadened so that I couldn't feel you. If I enlivened you, I felt my emotions more strongly and my pain emerged. If I numbed you, my memories remained buried; yet another self-distraction technique. I am sorry for those acts of misplaced aggression. I couldn't hold you safe because I had never been held safe. I had to first forge self-love in the fires of life.

I apologize for shaming you, loathing you, hiding you, feeling embarrassed about you. I am sorry that I judged your seeming imperfections as oddities rather than as reflections of the Godself. My attitude was a direct reflection of my own self-hatred, the internalized remnants of a shamed and vilified inner world. They told me I was ugly and I believed them. Characterized as the black sheep throughout my childhood, I took that message to heart, often perpetuating the shameathon at my own expense. As I work to bring my light out from under its bushel of shame, I see the wonder that is you shining through; such a majestic temple, a living prayer to the Godself. If we don't honor the temple, there will be no place to pray.

I apologize for looking for my spiritual life independent from you, as though God is a disembodied construct and not a felt experience. Like a good little head-tripper, I wanted to think God, rather than to feel God. And so I looked for God on the skyways of detachment, mistaking self-avoidance for enlightenment itself. I went down this path for some time, seemingly calm on the outside, but a bubbling cauldron of unresolved feelings in the deep within. In truth, the closest I ever came to an inclusive consciousness were in those moments when I surrendered to you completely, blemishes and all. It is no accident that we are here in physical form - God is IN the people. I apologize for looking for God outside the temple walls.

I apologize for weighing you down with physical and emotional armor: rigid musculature, congealed rage, shallowed breath, a hardened heart. Perfectly conditioned as a lone-wolf male warrior, I preferred solidity to fluidity, weaponry to warmth. A slave to survival, I was built to move along the path like a machine, postponing rest and pleasure for a day that seldom came. With my armor intact, nothing and no one could touch me. But I was borrowing energy from my future. I was killing myself. Even now, I am under no illusion that I will shift this way of being easily. It is deep in me, deep in my memories of overcoming. But I will try, one shedding at a time. I will try.

I apologize for subjecting you to objectified, heartsevered sexuality. You are built for intimacy that is depth-full, unifying, indistinguishable from the Godself. Anything less is a perversion of your divine nature. But I all too often wanted it shallow and Godless. I wanted no bridge between my heart and genitals, my heart and hers. Even when I was going through my 'tantra' phases, I was still abusing you, because I was using my genitals as a bliss seeking missile and not a bridge to the divine. I was using sexuality to escape the moment rather than to deepen in connection. I am sorry that I abused you in this way. I am committed to enheartening my sexuality. I am committed to building the heart-genital highway within.

I am grateful for the so many ways that you kept me going even when my waking consciousness was completely alienated from you. If I had been ruled by my thoughts alone, I would be long dead, bouncing as I was from one heady tree-top to another. But you never failed me, never forgot me, never lost sight of where I really lived. You kept breathing me when I acted against you, when I shamed you, when I disowned you. You kept loving me, calling me back, keeping me afloat until I could meet myself. Such devotion. Deep bows...

I am particularly grateful that you carried me through the most destructive life stages. You healed the wounds and broken bones of early life. You shielded me from violence with your fists and feet. You got me out of bed when grief was immobilizing my spirit. You pulled me out of the fires of childhood hell, even when I re-created them throughout adulthood. You warmed me up, as I knocked on thousands of doors to sell windows in frigid Canadian winters. You kept me awake through a sleepless trial law apprenticeship. You endured 3 decades of workaholism and over-compensation, with little rest. Dearest friend, how can I best honor you?

Thank you for being my authenticity-mometer, my temple of truth. How beautifully you carried my sacred purpose until I was ready for the hand-off. You reminded me with truth-chills whenever I walked in the right direction. You tripped me up with truth-aches whenever I dared to walk in someone else's shoes. What is so remarkable is that you never failed to communicate with me when I was living a lie. I may not have been ready to listen, but you never abandoned your faith in my possibilities. I now know that my true-path is encoded in the bones of my being. Not a temple that I visit, but one that I am.

I look forward to the day when humanity fully embraces your divinity and recognizes the unity at the heart of creation. A unified consciousness still exists outside of our habitual awareness, but it sings to us from deep within, a symphony of God-music that calls us home. Where body, mind and spirit may appear to be flowing in disparate directions, they will soon be revealed as inextricable branches of the same waterway. On the river of Essence, everything flows in the same direction — towards the ocean of wholeness.

As we move closer to a unified consciousness, may we recognize the heart of the matter- our enheartened body temple. Enlightenment is not a head trip- it's a heart trip, gusts of God blowing through the portal of the heart, the aortic love valve merging with the love that courses through the universal vein. As it turns out, it isn't beginner's mind we seek. Its' beginner's heart- the freshness of appreciation that flows through the open heart. If we want to expand our spiritual consciousness, we have to shake our heart tree often. Opening the heart unlocks the heart of the universe, and we see what is always before us. May we be committed to shedding the armor around our heart.

I am writing you by the banks of a small river, watching Canadian Geese land, resting and readying for the next leg of their journey south. I watch them, settling into a body they never left, truly here. Time to surrender, sing the birds of pray. Then, when their body is ready, they rise again, rising on the wings of their love. I hear them, calling out to each other. 'Surrender!', they cry, as they fly God home for the winter.

One day, I won't write you as though you are independent of my waking consciousness.

One day, I will pray to you, as you.

One day, I too will fly to God without leaving the temple.

Until then, please continue to hold me safe.

J.B., 2011

Growers are Inch Worms

I am often contacted by people who beat themselves up because they have not progressed on their spiritual journeys as quickly as they hoped. They are frustrated by their inability to embody their highest vision for themselves after only a few years, or even months, of determined effort. Quick fix, long suffering.

Today, I invite you to be patient with your path. The personal journey I wrote about in Soulshaping took me six years to write and 45 years to live. From the moment I began my first wave of psychotherapy until now is nearly 20 years. And, still, at the end of all that genuine effort, the trailways of transformation are no easy saunter. I still have a workaholic tendency, and a deep abandonment wound that arises when least expected.

This inspiration is a call to patience. Not the kind of patience that keeps us asleep (there are times when we need a karmic kick in the behind), but the kind that is compassionate and that sees our efforts to expand in a broader context. When my Grandfather would see me fail, he would see me with Grandpa eyes.

He would tell me that he loved me and remind me that those things I was attempting were not even imaginable when he was young. He recognized how extraordinary it was that I was considering a quest for my 'true-path,' only decades after he would have taken ANY path that paid the bills. This was a valuable teaching, and served me often when I developed superhuman expectations for myself. He taught me the meaning of context.

I invite us to honor our bravery. Given that most of the world is still vibrating around survivalism, the simple fact that we have formed the intention to transform our consciousness is already courageous. When we actually make a leap of faith and set sail for soulful waters, we have truly embarked on a heroic journey.

At the same time, let's not expect too much, too fast. However eager we may be, we will invariably turn back to familiar harbors to ground and protect ourselves. The fall back to our habitual range of emotion is a natural part of the journey home. Like turtles, we stick our heads out until it becomes uncomfortable and then retreat to the safety and familiarity of our shells. The time we spend under the shell can be just what we need to weave new experiences into our usual ways of being. So long as we persist in sticking our heads back out a little further each time, we continue to grow. Three steps forward, two steps back is still progress...

And we must also remember that REAL change simply takes time. Growers are inchworms. Lasting transformation is an incremental process, one 'soulstep' at a time. We can have all the peak experiences we want but the real work happens between the peaks, while lying down and integrating on the valley floor. This may frustrate us, but it is the only way to craft an awareness that is authentic and sustainable. Divine perspiration...

I remember a beautiful moment with my Grandmother before she died. She had often resisted my need to look at the past and deal with family baggage. It probably brought up her own unresolved memories. She often told me that I was involved in the therapeutic process for too long -- "Get on with it, Jeffrey." But, one day, she looked me in the eyes and said "You weren't just doing this for you, Jeffrey. You were also doing it for me. I couldn't look at these things in the world I lived in. You're healing my pain, too." And that said it all. Every step I took beyond the defenses and parameters of her world actually took my whole soulpod to the next level. All the more reason to take it slow. All the more reason to get it right.

The very fact that we are trying to heal our hearts in a world where so many have had to bury their hurt is already extraordinary. It may not seem like such a big deal, but when the energy has been moving in another direction for so many generations, it is quite a challenge to turn the tide. We are breaking new inner ground, after all. Recognizing this should translate into giving ourselves a break when we can't quite get it perfect. So let's see ourselves through Grandpa eyes, and breathe...

(from Jeff's ABC 'Good Morning America'
Inspiration collection- February 12, 2010)

Finding your Soulpod

As my spiritual journey deepened, friends fell away. As I shed one identity after another, I no longer identified with the people attached to them. It was as though the bridge between us had simply collapsed. Old ways of interacting seemed inauthentic, scripted, staged. We weren't walking down the same path anymore.

At first this suited me fine. With the quest for truth to keep me company, I didn't long for contact to fill me up or distract me from reality. My romance with my own soul engaged me more than most social experiences. Although there were some utterly lonely phases, I came to love my 'soulitude' -- undistracted time alone with my soul-self- because it was here that I met myself. It was in the heart of soulitude that I worked through many of my emotional obstructions and excavated the callings that lived within me. In its absence, I felt pulled back to old ways of being, and found it difficult to cultivate new possibilities. In an often overwhelming world, soulitude is essential to our efforts to clarify and transform.

What was interesting about my time alone was that I actually felt somewhat connected to all of humanity. The call to expand pulled me out of an isolated self-sense and reminded me that we are all part of the same interconnected web of connectiveness. Through these eyes, there were no strangers. We were all inextricably linked on the dance floor of sacred imagination.

After some time, I began to long for new friends to spend time with. Letting your soul be your pilot often means that you fly solo until you are ready for deeper connection. My time alone had been the perfect grist for my expansion, but now I needed real human contact. I had so many discoveries to share, and longed for people who could resonate with who I had become.

This is the nature of the self-creation journey. We move back and forth between polarities -- alone and connected, receptive and assertive, detached and attached -- until we find a way to integrate everything in a sacred balance. Now that I knew how to be alone, I needed to bring human sharing and intimacy back into the equation.

I began looking for my next 'soulpod' everywhere. Our soulpod is that person or group of people whom our soul finds the most resonance with at any given moment -- people of 'soulnificance.' It can include anyone that appears on our path to inform and catalyze our expansion -- our family of origin, significant figures, lovers, strangers with a lesson. How long they stay depends on the lesson. It could be a moment, a decade, a lifetime...

At first, my soulpod was very difficult to find. When I was less individuated, it had been easier to make friends. The more amorphous we are, the easier it is to find someone to have a drink with. But now I didn't want to just have a drink. I wanted to be met in the deep within. I wanted to connect with people walking the same soulbeat -- less ego, more essence, true to path.

And then they started to appear, in both expected and unexpected places. I found them at the yoga studios, the retreat centres, the hiking trails. But I also found them in taxis, at family gatherings (imagine that!) and even at the Thoroughbred racetrack. Ah, the sacred and the profane.

One member of my biological family crossed the bridge with me as well. My grandmother had been an essential figure in my birth pod, nourishing me amid the challenges of early life. Yet through new eyes I recognized that the vulnerable little woman at the head of my family was also a member of my consciousness pod. She too fought for the open heart within the distractions of daily life.

Inner growth is like a truth serum that reframes and clarifies our lens to the outside world. Our social life is one of the things that must change to accommodate our expansion and reflect our new ways of being. In this process, we must have faith that we will survive that often-lonely space between old friends falling away and new ones showing their face. This faith is our buffer against the temptation to go back to the familiar. If we can hang tight and make conscious efforts to connect, the next pod will be walked in our direction when the moment is right. We call to them, they call to us, and our angels broker the deal.

(from Jeff's ABC 'Good Morning America'
Inspiration collection- Dec. 22, 2010)

Befriending Confusion

Moving forward often demands that we live lost, knowingly surrendering our attachment to who we think we are, voluntarily stumbling around in the dark with little to guide us. Growing is all about leaps into the seeming unknown.

If there was one skill that I could not have done without on my spiritual journey, it was my learned capacity to befriend my confusion. As old ways of being died off, new ways of being invariably came to life. Before the transition was complete, there was a time, often a long time, when all of these parts were pressing up against me at the same time. In Soulshaping, I refer to this in-between phase as a "spiritual emergingcy" -- a state of confusion and inner tumult that arises when a new pathway is forcing its way into consciousness, prior to its full emergence and integration. The bridge from one side to the other is confusion. You have to learn how to hold the space for all of your parts and befriend your confusion, until clarity emerges on its own terms.

Unfortunately, befriending our confusion is difficult to sustain in a linear world. Those that walk the path of uncertainty are frequently characterized as flakes, drifters, and, ironically, lost souls. Nowhere in society are we taught to distinguish aimless from growth-full confusion, madness from truth aches, nervous breakdowns from nervous breakthroughs, habitual crisis from spiritual emergingcies. Confusion is sadly stigmatized as the mark of the "loser" without regard for the fact that one cannot come to know anything without first surrendering to the not knowing.

Our state of confusion often arises in the context of careers and relationships: Why do I hate my job? What are my callings? How do I really feel about this relationship? We develop a truth-ache- a sense of internal dissonance about our path, a crying out for another direction.

Sadly, when we begin questioning our choices, resistant voices often float to the surface -- voices of habit and fear, internalized judgments, well-entrenched defenses. Although progress has been made on many levels, most of us are still making our primary life-choices through a survivalist lens, with a vigilant eye to what is most practical, safe and materially satisfying.

When we step out of this framework, when we make a move toward a more soulful idea of success, we open the door to confusion, at least at first. The voices of the world arise within us in an effort to sweep away the whispers of a deeper truth. The desire to quit our unfulfilling job and find our callings is met with neurotic images of poverty. The longing to find a genuine soul-mate is overwhelmed with images of eternal aloneness. We are then confronted with a choice -- turn back to familiar harbors, or let the inner battle wage on. Play it safe, or see it through...

If we don't see it through, we risk all manner of difficulty. What ultimately holds us back is our resistance to bringing our truth ache into consciousness. Although sometimes painful, although it may well force us to turn our habitual patterns upside down, the truth-ache contains the seeds of our transformation. When we repress it, truth-decay sets in, and the only thing that can save us is a truth canal. Sometimes we wait too long, and we lose our truth altogether.

But if you can see it all the way through, you will be rewarded. You will know a measure of soul-satisfaction that you will never know on a false path. You will see through different eyes and feel at peace in your soul-skin. You will not have to ask the universe for what you need because the door to humanifestation will open wide as the universe rewards you for your courage. You will know a remarkably enriched reality.

(from Jeff's ABC 'Good Morning America' Inspiration collection- Dec. 22, 2010)

Boundaries, boundaries, boundaries:
Don't leave home without them

I grew up in a home without boundaries. We had walls between the rooms, and locks on the bathroom doors, but there were no relational boundaries between us. With our consciousness overwhelmed by emotional and economic challenges, there was no space to consider notions of healthy relating. 'Survival at all costs' was our daily mantra. Like wild animals, we were either huddled together for dear life, or fighting one another for scraps. Healthy boundaries were a subtle consideration, a luxury that we simply could not afford.

This imbalanced way of being carried forward to my intimate relationships. Either I co-dependently fused with my partners, or I put on my emotional armor and ran away. My habitual range of emotion. Not surprisingly, my methods of detachment were identical to what was modeled to me as a child. Moments of closeness were inevitably followed by intensity and conflict. Back and forth between enmeshment and war -- what else did I know? And of course, conflict was far more than just habitual. It was also avoidant. There was no better way to avoid genuine vulnerability than being at war.

After 15 years of psychotherapy, I finally came to appreciate the profound significance of healthy boundaries in every area of life. As a general rule, if we are too rigid, we are over-boundaried. Imprisoned behind a wall of armor, there is no way for anything to touch us. But if we are too malleable, we are boundary-less. We are just a vessel for the world to fill.

People with healthy boundaries tend to live somewhere in between. They have found the sacred balance between assertiveness and receptivity. When they do move toward one polarity, they do so with intentionality. They choose to surrender, choose to assert. In all cases, their sense of self remains intact.

This is particularly important in our relationship lives. If we don't know where we end and the other begins, we will have a difficult time establishing healthy connections. Those of us with weakly formed boundaries will be easily manipulated and influenced, often confusing our partner's feelings for our own. Those of us with hardened boundaries will have a hard time opening our hearts to love. Our walls are simply too thick to penetrate. The sacred balance is an alchemical blend of structure and fluidity, almost like an open heart with a sturdy gate at the opening. We don't let just anyone in. We selectively open, letting our boundaries down only when we know that it is healthy to do so.

Healthy boundaries are also significant in our spiritual lives. On my Soulshaping journey, this has been my greatest area of confusion with boundary formation. For the longest time, I sought an experience of 'all-oneness' that transcended the boundaried, separate self. I didn't want to be Jeff, I didn't want to be from my family, I didn't want to deal with my individual challenges.

This vision of possibility was fueled by certain experiences that I had on the meditation mat and in my emotional healing work. At times, I was able to tap into a vaster field of consciousness than my habitual sensibilities. This comforted me, both because it gave me a break from my anxious imaginings and because it provided me with a glimpse into a more unified way of being. A rare break from the madness of the world.

Unfortunately, I misunderstood the nature of the interface between my separate self and unity consciousness. It is one thing to distinguish ourselves from limiting dualities, but quite another to eradicate the distinct self altogether. When taken too far, the quest for 'All-One' can become a recipe for radical detachment and perilous self-avoidance. After some time floating away from life's challenges, I came crashing down to Earth. Without a self to come home to, my forays into unity were ultimately unsustainable. It seems I had forgotten to take care of my economic reality and to tend to my primary relationships. I was soon reminded. This is the nature of karmic gravity. If we don't ascend with both feet on the ground, reality will always bring us back to earth to remind us.

There is a sacred balance between our experience of unity consciousness and our connection to our individual path in the heart of it -- separate voices inextricably woven through a choir of unified light. The more deeply we grow in our individual spirituality, the more genuine is our experience of unity. To let go of duality, we must first establish our separateness. To truly taste from unity, we must learn where we end and the other begins. Boundaries, boundaries, boundaries. Don't leave home without them.

(from Jeff's ABC 'Good Morning America'
Inspiration collection- April 8, 2011)

Dear Dad

It is finally our time. To heal these mortal rifts. To remember each other. We couldn't do it until now. Liberated from your pain riddled earth-suit, I can feel you again. I am no longer afraid to get close. I know you won't hurt me now. You have freed me to love you again. In fact, I feel you protecting me. Already. That purple sunset, that's you right? That strengthening I feel inside- that's you too, yes? You are speaking to me, through me. You are hearticulating your love. You have much to share. I understand- it was hard to say it then, with all that mortal pain between. But I can hear you, Papa. There's nothing in the way now. No more hatred, no more misidentification, no more fear of showing our love. Nothing to hide, nowhere to hide it. Here we are, on the bridge between our hearts, beginning the healing. We have work to do. A lot of it. This is only our first purple sunset.

It's an odd thing. I was sure I would abuse myself for being so distant for so long. I should have done this, or that, I should have visited more. But something has happened. I am treasuring myself. Suddenly the shame game looks ridiculous. Something more infinite is infiltrating my lens. Is that you, too? You are sending waves of kindness my way? It's you, isn't it? Your anger is gone- all I feel is your compassionate heart. You are speaking through me: "You must love yourself, my son. You must embody your magnificence. There is no need to doubt it. I am sorry that I shamed you".

I need your support now. I have much left to do in my earth suit. I hope you will clear the path. I hope you will keep the dark forces at bay. Your call to write lives on in me. It was never lost. You loved it forward. I will write for you, too. The world didn't know what greatness you are made of. But I do.

Please hold me safe until it is my time to join you, Dad. One day I will meet you there, in the wordless wonder. One day we will heal it all, in the ever knowing. One day we will ride together on the wings of our love. In the meantime, rest in love, Albert Ronald Brown. I am holding your spirit safe, too.

(published on Soulshaping.com on July 6, 2013)

Let there be love.

♡

.

About the Author

Born in Toronto, Canada, Jeff Brown did all the things he was supposed to do to become successful in the eyes of the world. He was on the Dean's Honor List as an undergraduate. He won the Law and Medicine prize in law school. He apprenticed with top criminal lawyer Eddie Greenspan. It had been Jeff's lifelong dream to practice criminal law and search for the truth in the courtroom.

But then, on the verge of opening a law practice, he heard a little voice inside telling him to 'stop, just stop.' With great difficulty, he honored this voice and began a heartfelt quest for the truth that lived within him. Although he didn't realize it at the time, Jeff was actually questing for his innate image, the essential being that he came into this lifetime to embody. He was searching for his authentic face, his sacred purpose, his true-path.

As part of his journey, he explored many possible paths. He studied Bioenergetics and did session work with co-founder Alexander Lowen. He practiced as a body-centered psychotherapist and completed an MA in Psychology at Saybrook Graduate School in San Francisco. He also co-founded the Open Heart Gang, a benevolent gang with a heartfelt intention. Their first creation—the emotionally riveting and unforgettable spiritual documentary "Karmageddon"—is now complete. The film, which focuses on Jeff's journey with chanter and spiritual teacher Bhagavan Das, includes engaging interviews with Jeff and author Ram Dass, yogis Seane Corn and David Newman, and chanters Robert Gass, Wah, Deva Premal and Miten. It won the Audience Choice Award at the Costa Rica International Film Festival in 2012.

In 2001, Jeff was overwhelmed by the need to write. It was strong and it was determined, a soulnami of sacred purpose that absolutely had to be expressed if he was to have any peace. This is the nature of a calling once it has been awakened. After six years of arduous work, his first book—*Soulshaping*: *Adventures in Self-Creation*—was published in 2007. A candid and personal autobiographical exploration, *Soulshaping* caught fire immediately. This fire was further fueled by a homeless man called Slim who sold the book on the streets of Toronto. Seeing Slim successfully sell hundreds of copies planted a seed of possibility in Jeff's mind that would eventually become the *Love It Forward* movement.

Soulshaping was later contracted to North Atlantic Books and re-published in August, 2009 with a new sub-title—*Soulshaping: A Journey of Self-Creation*. Soon thereafter, Jeff began writing inspirations for ABC's Good Morning America. He was interviewed by CNN radio, appeared on Fox News.com, and wrote articles for the Washington Post's On Faith blog and Vivid Life.

In September, 2010, Jeff wrote a blog called "Apologies to the Divine Feminine—from a warrior in transition," which was met with a viral response on Facebook and beyond. Since then, Apologies has been translated and re-printed countless times.

In October, 2012, Jeff published his first book of spiritual graffiti called *Ascending with Both Feet on the Ground: Words to Awaken your Heart.*

Love It Forward is his second book of spiritual graffiti.

At present, Jeff is living just outside of Toronto, where he is writing a higher consciousness love story and beginning a new career as founder of the publishing house Enrealment Press. He is also working hard to expand his new heart-centered movement—*Love It Forward* (LIF)—which launched in October, 2013. This book reflects the benevolent intentionality at its heart.

www.soulshaping.com
www.loveitforward.net
www.karmageddonthemovie.net